MW01680304

GOLF MAGIC

Your Magical Guide To Better Golf

By Carlino Giampolo

Published by
Carlino & Company
P.O. Box 15182
Honolulu, Hawaii 96830
(808) 926-1752

Copyright 2005 Carlino Giampolo

All Rights Reserved

This book may not be reproduced in whole or in part, except by written permission from the publisher.

ISBN: 0-937827-01-0

First Printing September 2005

Design, typography and print production by
Blaine Fergerstrom, ZZ Type, zztype.com

There are many sources available for you to explore and expand your personal magic. One such source is: Concept: Synergy, P.O. Box 691867, Orlando, Florida 32869.

You may purchase additional copies of this book at:

www.GolfMagic.us

Visit our other Web Sites at:
www.BeliefsWithoutBorders.com
www.TheArtOfLettingGo.com
www.TheLandOfAloha.com
www.Carlino.us

***Golf Magic** is a sharing of my personal experiences as a beginner golfer.* The purpose of the book is to help the reader become more successful at playing golf and to have more fun.

Although this book is intended for the beginning golfer, its contents can also help those who are already familiar with the game of golf.

***Golf Magic** will challenge some beliefs about golf that have been popular for centuries.* Also, some of the techniques discussed, such as that for the alignment, may be very different from what is usually taught. As with all books of this nature, absorb the contents, then filter out what is useful to you for your improvement and allow that to become a part of your game.

Finally, don't compare yourself to others. Know yourself and what works for you. There is no "one and only" way to play the game of golf.

It is my hope that this book will become invaluable in helping you to achieve your golf dreams and to discover your own personal golf magic.

Note: The book is written for a right-handed golfer. A left-handed golfer would make reference to the opposite indications when appropriate.

Acknowledgements

My sincerest thanks to the many professional and non-professional golfers who gave of their wisdom and talent to help me in my beginning years as a golfer. Especially to *Ralphie G. Cekay*, who was my first inspiration to begin playing golf.

Also, a special thanks to the many professional and non-professional golfers whose willing expertise and suggestions were of great assistance in the completion of this book.

I am grateful to the following people whose images are used for illustrating the text:

Bobby Acoba, Aileen Batungbacal, Gary Batungbacal, Jehu Fuller, Junko Honma, Bobby Jewell, Brent Jurgenson, Norman Nakamoto, Rob Nelson, Gary Peterson, Chris Pliska, Alexis Scalise, Russell Tang, Tamaki Torre, John Tsukamoto, Jim Winpenny, and Frank Zakimi.

Also, my deepest gratitude to *Dr. James Cascaito* and *Jim Winpenny* for their editorial assistance and keen insight, and to *Blaine Fergerstrom* for his production skills.

Finally, this book is dedicated to my *immediate family* – the living treasure in my life – for standing by me in all of my endeavors.

Table of Contents

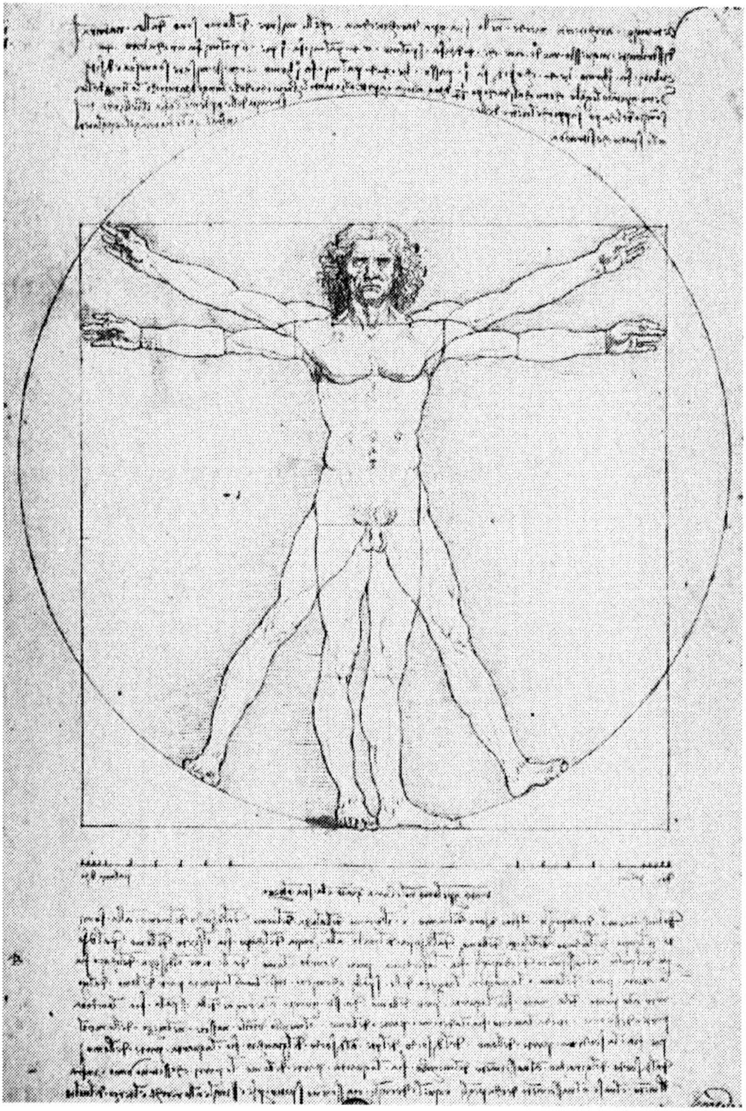

Vitruvian by Leonardo da Vinci.

Stretching and Warm-up

It is deceiving to think that golf is not a truly physical sport. To play your best golf and to help prevent injuries while playing, your body needs to be strong and flexible.

Therefore, before practicing or playing a round of golf you should take time to do stretching and warm-up exercises. The time invested in doing so is well worth it in terms of your health and performance.

Many players' performances improve as their rounds of golf progress. That is due in part to the fact that their bodies have become more flexible. Stretch and warmup before starting your round or practice session in order to be at your optimum performance level from the very beginning.

The most serious physical problems for golfers are injuries to their backs and knees so be most aware of those areas of your body. Many professionals do weight training as part of their conditioning program and you can do that if you feel it is necessary. The main criterion is that you be aware of what your body needs in order to stay healthy for playing this game.

The following pages in this section have examples of a few exercises you can do before starting your round of golf or practice session.

Stretching and Warm-up

1) Place your hands on the club shaft slightly beyond shoulder-width apart and then rest the club on your shoulders.

2) With your feet shoulder-width apart and knees flexed, turn your shoulders to the right as far as you can comfortably go. Keep your head forward. Hold for 10 seconds.

Repeat to the left side.

Do several repetitions.

Stretching and Warm-up

1) Hold the club at each end. Place the club parallel to the ground and directly in front of you at waist level.

Place your feet shoulder-width apart. Flex your knees and bend forward slightly from the waist.

2) Dip your left shoulder down and turn your shoulders to the right as far as you can comfortably go. Hold for 10 seconds. Make certain your head stays forward and doesn't turn with your body.

Repeat to the left side.

Do several repetitions.

Stretching and Warm-up

Hold the club head with your left hand. Place the bottom of the club shaft on the ground in front of you an arm's length away so that the club shaft is perpendicular to the ground.

Place your right hand on your right foot and bend your right leg behind you. Hold for 10 seconds.

Now hold the club with your right hand and repeat the exercise for your left leg.

Do several repetitions.

Stretching and Warm-up

Take two clubs and swing back and through to your finish position. Repeat for 20 times.

Then take the club you will be using on the first tee or will be first practicing with and swing it back and through as normal for 10 times.

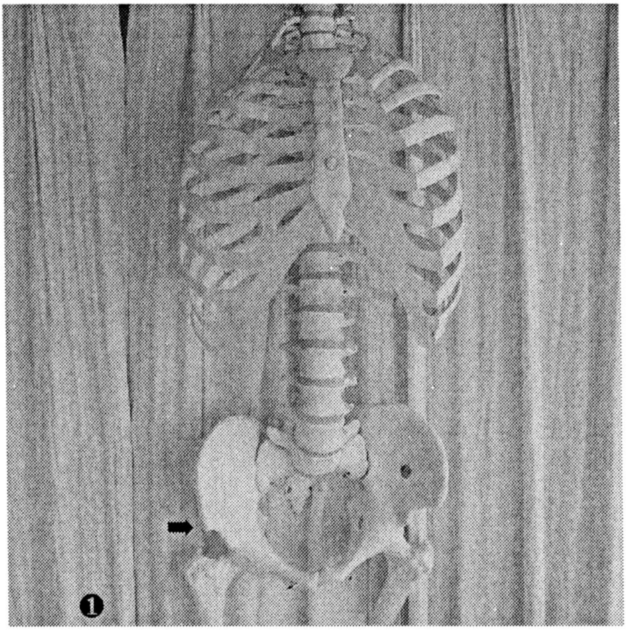

The Author's Alignment Method

Proper alignment is the foundation — and the most important fundamental element — of your swing. Many swing errors can be traced to a faulty alignment. If you are not aligned properly you will not be able to produce the results you want.

The most important fundamental part of your body that must be in alignment is your pelvis. By having your pelvic area in alignment you are in a good position to have your shoulders, hips and feet in alignment, as well as increasing your power.

So begin your set-up routine by developing the proper pelvic alignment. And do so by going to the practice range and developing the feel for proper pelvic alignment.

1) ***The main pelvic bone is approximately one inch below your belly button and to both sides. It is directly above the middle of each leg.*** Hold your club horizontally and place the bottom of the shaft on your right pelvic bone. Move your foot from right to left in a steady motion. Notice how the club shaft changes direction as you do so.

Be aware of the interaction between your feet and your pelvis. Twist your right foot completely to the left and hold it there, being aware of your pelvic position. If you tried to swing a club from this position, you would be swinging outside-in toward the ball and most likely would slice the ball to the right.

The Author's Alignment Method

2) Use your driver and tee up the ball with half of the ball above the top of the clubhead and half below it. Place another club in front of the ball in a direct line from the ball to the target. *This is the target line.*

3) ***With your driver in hand, stand about two feet behind the ball with the club shaft on your right pelvic bone parallel to the ground.*** Start with your pelvis and right foot flared to the right, then turn your pelvis until your driver is in alignment with the club that is in front of the ball. *Take a moment to visualize the path your ball will take to the target.*

4) ***To begin the process of having your body in alignment with your target line, place your driver on your left pelvis bone and hold it parallel to the ground.*** With your left foot parallel and against your right foot, move your left foot approximately two feet directly across to your left side.

(Because you are using a driver — which is the longest club in your bag — you will be moving your left foot this distance. If you were using a shorter club, like a 9-iron, you would be moving your left foot only about one foot to the side. As you continue to practice this simple alignment method it will become easy for you to determine what distance to move your left foot for your various clubs.)

5) Notice the direction of the shaft. Now imagine a line extended from your shaft to about six feet in front of you. *This is your body line and the line direction you will want your pelvis to be in alignment with.*

6

8

The Author's Alignment Method

Do a simple step and turn to get your pelvis in alignment with this direction, as follows.

6) ***Cross your right foot over to where it is in front of your left foot and across from the ball. You will notice that your right foot is also facing the same direction as your imaginary line.***

6a) Turn your body to the right until it is in alignment with this imaginary line.

7) A simple check is to place the club shaft against your pelvis and see if it is in alignment with your body line.

8) ***To continue practicing with this important alignment position, place another club on this body line about four feet in front of you.***

9) *The correct body alignment when addressing the ball is when your target line and body line are parallel.* Some imagine it as being railroad tracks with one track to the target which is your target line and one track to the left of the target which is your body line.

The Author's Alignment Method

10) ***Next, center your clubhead behind the ball and put it in square alignment with your target line.***

11) ***Imagine one line across the front of your feet. And another from your clubhead to your feet. The line from your clubhead should be perpendicular to the line across the front of your feet.***

12) ***You are now in the proper alignment. The target line and body line are parallel to each other. And the clubhead is in square alignment with your target line and perpendicular to your body.***

For a beginner it is easier and best to have your body in alignment first and then your clubhead in line with your body, rather than squaring your clubhead to the target first and then aligning your body to the clubhead.

When you have first aligned your body properly, the clubhead, when placed naturally behind the ball, will be in the proper alignment with your target line and perpendicular to your body.

And it is easy to make an adjustment. If you feel your clubhead is in alignment with your target line but not perpendicular to your body, then turn your whole body slightly to the right or left until your body is perpendicular to your clubhead.

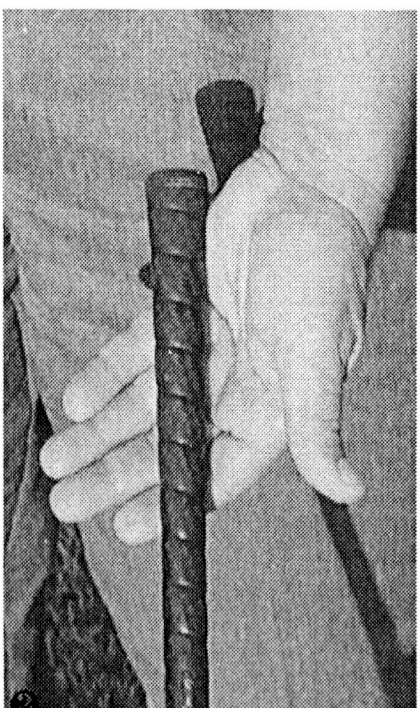

The Grip

There are several different ways to grip a club and you will have to determine which one is best for you.

1) ***One of the methods used is the baseball grip, used primarily by individuals wth small hands who feel this kind of grip can give them more power. It is sometimes referred to as the ten-finger grip because all ten fingers are touching the club.*** It is similar to the interlocking grip discussed below except that the index finger of the left hand is on the shaft and does not interlock with the bottom two fingers of the right hand.

One of the most popular grips, and the one I feel gives me better control of the club, is the interlocking grip which is a variation of the Vardon or overlapping grip.

2) ***To use this grip, place the handle of the club in your left hand between the first and second joints of your index and middle fingers, and let it rest at the base of the other two fingers. Close your hand.***

3) ***Your left thumb can be either on the center line of the handle or right of center. When you look down you should be able to see the first two or three knuckles of your left hand.***

❹

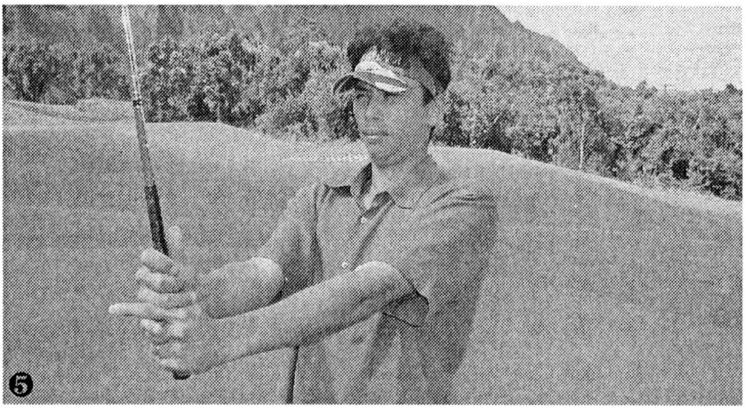

❺

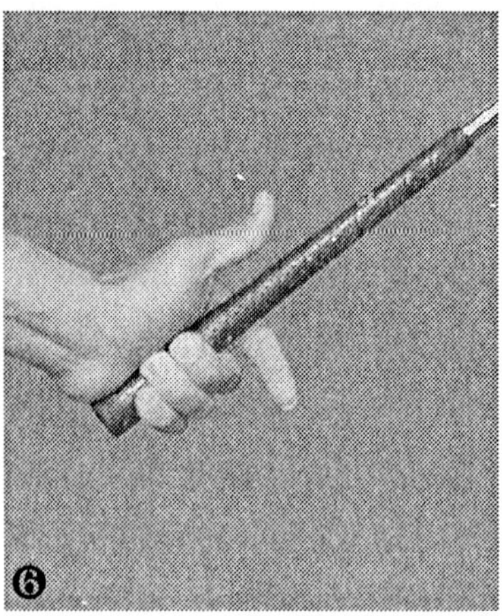

❻

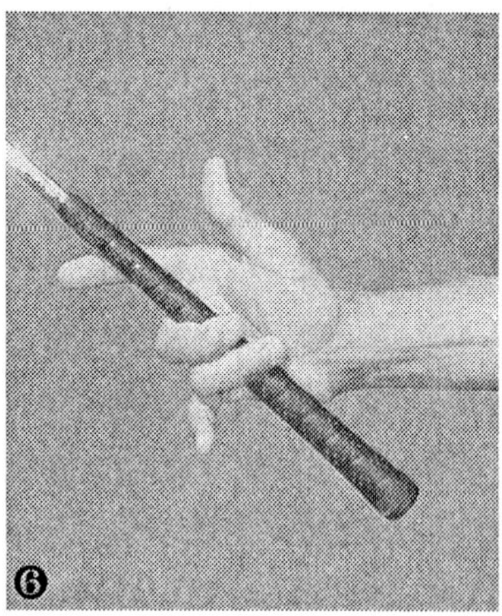

❻

The Grip

4) ***Slide your right hand down the handle at the base of your finger joints.***

5) ***The index finger of the left hand interlocks with the bottom two fingers of the right hand.*** Close your fingers. The right thumb is resting slightly to the left of the center of the handle, and the left thumb is in the palm of the right hand. The "V" of your right hand formed by the thumb and index finger points between your chin and right shoulder. The index finger and thumb of the right hand exert light pressure on the club similar to the squeezing of a trigger.

6) ***Your club is held mainly with the bottom three fingers of the left hand and the middle two fingers of the right hand. These are your strong pressure points.***

Your grip pressure should be firm but not tight. Too much grip pressure produces tension in the arms. On a scale of 1-10 with 10 being the most pressure, your grip pressure should be somewhere from 5-7. If you were to hold the club up in the air someone should be able to pull the club out of your hand, but with some resistance.

When you go to the practice range you should hit several shots with a very loose grip and then with a very tight grip. Be aware of what went wrong with your shot due to improper grip pressure.

Distance from Ball

Where you stand in relation to the ball is critical to a successful shot. Being too close or too far away from the ball will not give you the result you want.

1) ***Begin by developing the proper spine angle. You don't want to be too upright or too crouched over. One of the easiest and best ways to develop the proper spine position and distance from the ball is to stand straight, take a deep breath, and pretend you are about to sit down on the edge of a high stool that is a couple of inches beneath you.***

You will notice that you are bent over from the hips and there is a slight bend to your knees. Your weight is slightly more on the balls and middle part of your feet — not on the toes or heels. Your spine is straight from the back of your neck to the tailbone.

2) ***For most golfers, a check to determine the correct distance from the ball is obtained when the top of the club's handle is about a hand's width away from the body.*** You should be able to make a fist and move your fist across your body, lightly touching your body and the top of the club shaft. However, if you have a large build, the distance between your fist and body may be several inches.

3) *Most importantly, though, when you grip the club, your hands are in a position where they are hanging down naturally in front of your body — neither too far stretched out nor cramped in against your body.*

Feet Position

This feet-position technique is one that I use for the majority of my shots and found it most advantageous for having the ball in the proper position.

1) ***With your body properly aligned, feet together and the clubhead square to the target line, let the shaft rest naturally. Move your body slightly to the right or left until the shaft of the club is in the center of your body.***

2) ***Now move your left foot straight across approximately three to five inches to the left. (This distance will depend on your body size.) Most importantly, the ball on the ground should be in line with the middle of the left side of your chest. And your hands are in front of the ball.***

3) ***Place your right foot underneath your right shoulder.*** Because of the greater distance you are moving your right foot, be aware that it is moving directly across and not forward or backward. Moving the right foot improperly can result in an improper body line.

Your head is behind the ball and the left shoulder is slightly higher than the right shoulder.

For most shots, your right foot would be underneath your right shoulder. However, you can move your right foot farther beyond your right shoulder if you want to increase your distance, or not as close to your right shoulder for short shots, in order to have better balance and control.

Breath

The final component of your set-up routine before you begin your backswing is that of breath control.

People who study martial arts are well aware of how breath control can increase their strength and place them more in a position of total control. They understand its benefits both physically and mentally. *These benefits also hold true for golf.*

1) ***Take a deep breath and hold it about two inches below your navel.***

Proper breath control can:

A) Give you more stability.

B) Increase your power.

C) Help you to relax and reduce the tightness of your muscles.

D) Help you to develop a more rhythmic swing.

E) Help you to focus on what you want to accomplish with your swing.

Set-up Routine

1) Alignment

2) The Grip

3) Distance from Ball

4) Feet Position

5) Breath

Review

You should develop the habit of a pre-shot routine every time you plan to execute a shot.

This is important to do because many times a bad shot can be traced to the set-up rather than a faulty swing. And although you may think your swing has to improve, it could very well be that your swing is fine but you have to improve one of the components of your set-up routine.

So before changing your swing or becoming frustrated with your game, go back and review the basics of your set-up routine.

Backswing

The golf swing consists of a coiling and uncoiling of your body.

To simplify the basics of the backswing, I have found it beneficial to separate it into two steps – the first step is bringing the club directly across to your right side, and the second is having your back facing the target line.

First Step - Think "Rounded Shoulders"

Start your takeaway of the club with the singular thought of "rounded shoulders." This thought was very helpful to me in having my club, hands, arms, chest and shoulders move away together as a singular unit, rather than using only my arms to take the club back.

It is very important in the first few inches of taking the club away that the clubhead moves straight back, square to your target line and low to the ground. If you don't begin correctly, most likely you will not end correctly.

1) ***Perform your takeaway by turning your shoulders to the right in a rounded motion and stop it when the clubhead is directly across your body and near eye level. Your hands will be just below chest level.***

This singular thought of "rounded shoulders" will also prevent you from taking the club back too far to the inside which is a frequent mistake of beginners.

Backswing

You want to take the club back in a wide motion in the first part of your backswing. And by putting the clubhead near eye-level you will be capable of a more powerful swing.

Notice the graphic on the opposite page:

A) The arms in this position are across the front of your chest, but not rigidly straight. They are slightly below being parallel to the ground.

B) The wrists break naturally. The wrist cock is built into your swing. Don't think about doing anything with your wrists.

C) The clubhead is pointing straight up, not to the left or right.

D) If someone were standing to your right, he or she would be able to see the middle of your chest due to the turning of your body.

E) Your weight will go in the direction of the club. The weight has now shifted to the inside of the right foot. Keep the weight in this inside position; don't allow it to extend beyond this point.

Backswing

Notice the graphic on the opposite page:

F) Your right knee is slightly flexed, the same flex position as in your set-up.

G) Your right leg is solid. It doesn't sway to the right side.

H) Your hips have turned into your right leg. This is not a shifting motion.

I) Your head has moved slightly behind the ball because of its connection to the movement of your shoulders. Your head does not have to be rigidly still but you also don't want to have excessive head movement.

J) If you let the shaft of your club fall toward you, it should hit you on the tip of your right shoulder.

1

Backswing

Now let's complete the backswing.

Second Step – Think "Back to the Target."

From this first step position simply think "back to the target." You want to turn your back into a position where it is facing your target. *This thought helped me to be in a position to have the ball go farther and straighter.* Remember that the longer the club, the more you need to turn your back to the target.

1) ***Begin the "back to the target" thought with your left shoulder dropping down underneath your chin and turn your back to the target. Take the club back naturally and stop it when the clubhead is facing left of the target.*** You can see how this part of your swing coincides with the importance of the stretching exercises we talked about earlier.

This thought will also help prevent your right arm from moving away from your body.

You will notice that the big muscles in the trunk of your body, together with your arms, will help you to complete this second half of your swing. *This is another reason why your pelvis and the rest of your body must be in proper alignment.*

Backswing

Look at the graphic on the opposite page:

A) The shoulders have turned a full 90 degrees.

B) The left shoulder is to the right of the ball. The right shoulder is directly behind the head.

C) The right elbow forms an "L" shape.

D) The clubhead is pointing to the left of the target.

E) The back of the left hand is at the same angle as the clubhead.

F) The body weight is still on the inside of the right foot.

G) The left heel has lifted and is slightly off the ground.

Downswing

Think "Left Heel Down."

The downswing begins from the ground up. It begins with the left heel down if you lift your left heel on the backswing. If you don't lift your left heel on the backswing, then a shift of weight onto your left heel begins the process.

1) ***By initiating your downswing with your left heel down, you allow the left side of your body to be out of the way, making it easier for you to unwind your body in one synchronized motion.*** Your weight has shifted to your left leg and your left hip has begun to rotate to the left. Your left knee and hip have turned out of the way.

2) ***After your left heel is down, pull the club straight down with your hands.*** Trust your body to swing the arms, hands, and clubhead through the ball.

3) As you continue your downswing:

A) The right arm stays close to the body.

B) The head remains behind the ball.

C) The left side of the body is out of the way.

D) The belt buckle is in front of the hands.

Downswing

The graphic on the opposite page shows the "*impact zone*," which is about 12 inches behind the ball:

A) The left arm is straightening at the impact zone.

B) The clubhead is square to the target line.

C) The left leg is *straight.*

D) The head is behind the ball.

E) The arms are in front of the right side of the body and not behind it.

Downswing

The graphic on the opposite page shows the follow through:

A) The club will swing through the ball, not at the ball.

B) 90 percent of the body weight is on the left foot. The right foot is up on its toes.

C) The hands are directly atop the left shoulder.

D) The front of the body, including the right shoulder, is facing the target.

E) The finish is held until the ball has landed.

1

1

The Swing

1) ***The swing basics have been separated into various components, but your actual swing will be one continuous, fluid motion.***

You can hold only one thought at a time when you swing, so determine which thought works best for you. "Rounded shoulders," "back to the target," "left heel down," "swing through the ball," "hold the finish": these are a few suggestions. Or you may want to think of nothing at all. This is something very personal. *You must decide what produces the best results for you.*

Golf is as much about feeling as it is about technique. From your set-up position an effective technique is to take a slow backswing and downswing stopping about 6 inches from the ball. If you feel uncomfortable, or if the club is not moving through smoothly, then you will need to make an adjustment.

From your set-up position, for example, your right foot may have to be moved slightly forward or back for a smoother downswing. Or you may want to move your left foot slightly toward your target to create a freer movement in your pelvic area. Or you may have too much of your weight on the left side of your body. Or your alignment may be off.

In order to utilize your acquired knowledge effectively you will need to practice and develop your ability to feel and know what adjustments you have to make.

Rhythm

You will have to develop a rhythm to your swing that will result in one fluid motion. You don't want to stop and then continue your motion. You want to develop your feel for a smooth back-and-forth motion.

You can hit the ball only so far. The tempo (how fast you swing and your maximum speed at impact) is something you can develop on the practice range.

1) ***One technique is to place five golf balls on the ground and to begin by hitting as easy as you can and then increasing your speed for each successive ball.*** You will see that the optimal speed for you will be somewhere between hitting as easy and as hard as you can.

Remember that it is primarily the rotation of your pelvis area and knees that aids greater distance.

Be aware of your speed on your backswing. Taking the club back fast will not help you to achieve any greater distance. Take a backswing which is slower than that of your downswing.

Your power will also come from the speed of your downswing. This is similar to what baseball players do. They take a slow back swing and a faster forward swing.

Create the feeling of knowing the optimum rhythm and speed for you.

Long Game

1) ***The long game is more important than the short game!!! That belief is based upon my own personal experiences and observations.***

The opposite belief – that the short game is more important than the long game – has been in existence for centuries and is deeply ingrained in the mindset of the golfing community. It is a belief based more on the abilities of the professional rather than on those of the beginner.

There are three separate games in golf: putting, long game, and short game. Putting is the most important and will be discussed later. *Next is the long game, 150 yards and beyond for males, and 110 yards and beyond for females.* And then there is the short game, which is less than 150 yards for males and less than 110 yards for females.

If you have only one hour to practice, you should use 30 minutes for putting, 20 minutes for the long game and 10 minutes for the short game.

Remember that belief precedes experience. If you believe your long game is more difficult to master than your short game, then you are going to create that kind of reality.

You must develop the belief that you can be successful in your long game as well as in your short game and in putting.

Long Game

1) ***Have confidence in your ability to execute your long game as easily as you can your short game.***

If you are a male, you will be playing from the resort tees at most golf courses, ***and if you can develop the ability to hit your drives in the 200-220 yard range,*** you will find that most of your second shots will be in the range of 150-190 yards for the par 4's. For par 3's you will use both your long and short game. And for par 5's your second and third shots will be your long game.

If you are a female, you will be playing from the forward tees, ***and if you can develop the ability to hit your drives in the 160-180 yard range***, you will find that most of your second shots will be in the 110-150 yard range for the par 4's. And, like the men, for the par 3's you will use both your long and short game, and for par 5's your second and third shots will be your long game.

So, it is vitally important that you have confidence in your ability to be successful in your long game.

If your first two shots on a par 4 are executed successfully, then you will be putting for birdie. And, if you can execute your first two shots successfully the majority of the time, you will be using your short game only when you don't execute the long game the way you desire.

Increase Power

There are several techniques and options available for helping you to increase power for your long game.

Here are a few of them:

1) To get an additional 10 yards or more on your golf shots, move your right foot a couple of inches more to the right when you setup, and play the ball slightly forward in your stance, near your left instep.

2) ***By turning your back to the target in your back-swing you increase the rotation of your body and the centrifugal force it generates through impact.*** You will find that the more flexibility you have in turning your back to the hole, the farther and straighter the ball will travel.

3) Discover the speed of your swing. Generally speaking, the faster you swing the club, the greater the distance you will get. But don't try to swing the fastest you can. You have to swing within your own range by experimenting as to what is the optimum speed for you.

4) Physically, you can increase your strength and flexibility with stretching exercises and strength conditioning.

Increase Power

5) ***By using your entire body in your swing, especially the pelvis area which is a part of the biggest muscle group, you can exert tremendous force at the point of impact.*** Someone once asked Babe Ruth: "Where do you get the power to hit so many home runs?" His answer: "I hit the ball with my stomach."

6) You can add extra yardage by extending your swing to a complete, balanced finish.

7) The proper equipment is also important. Sometimes changing a club can give you an additional 20-30 yards or more. Experiment with different clubs to know which ones produce the best results for you.

8) Certain golf balls can also help you to increase your yardage. Again, experiment to discover which ones are best for you.

9) You must have breath control in your set-up. Never underestimate the power of your breath. Martial artists are keenly aware of its value and so should you be.

10) There is power in your feet. Be aware of the positioning of your feet and the distribution of your weight, especially on your back and forward swings.

Short Game

It was mentioned earlier that the long game is more important than the short game. *This in no way diminishes the value and importance of the short game.*

The short game can help you to recover from an errant long game; and being skillful at the short game will greatly improve your score.

Here are some *suggestions* for your short game:

1) ***I found that it is best for a beginner to become adept at using two clubs for the short game – a lofted and a less-lofted club.*** For example, you may decide to use a 9-iron and a 7-iron for your short game. Or you may decide on a pitching wedge and a 6-iron, or a sand wedge and an 8-iron. Experiment with various clubs to determine which two clubs work best for you. After your game progresses you can add additional clubs for your short game. For now, it's more important that you are confident and skillful with these two types of clubs. *It is more important as a beginner that you become proficient at using these two types of clubs rather than being mediocre using a variety of clubs.*

2) *Practice using both clubs from the same distance. Take notice of the trajectory of the ball and the distance the ball rolls for each club.* You will notice that the more-lofted club such as a 9-iron will travel higher and have less roll on the green, than a 7-iron which will have a lower trajectory and more roll on the green.

Short Game

3) *Practice at first by beginning from 50 yards and in.* This will be the area where the majority of your long shots will fall short.

4) ***Here's a simple technique to determine how far back to bring your club: Imagine a golf ball in your hand. How far back would you have to take your arm if you were to throw the ball underhand onto the green?*** You can practice this technique with the club in your hand; this immediately gets you into the position of where you will know how far back the club will go.

5) Use the above technique to determine also the speed at which you will take the club back. Remember to keep that same speed going forward. *Don't decelerate on your downswing.*

6) Even though your swing is shorter, you must be certain that your swing mechanics are sound. *The two areas to concentrate on most are: turning your shoulders on the backswing, and shifting the weight to your left foot on the downswing.* Most short shots are errant when the club is taken back with the arms only and when the weight stays on the right foot.

7) *Two other key areas for concentration are: to make sure your hands are ahead of the ball, and to keep your head down until you have finished your swing.*

8) *Maintain a strong, positive mental attitude.* For your short game, think "one and one." One shot to get onto the green, and one to putt.

Sand Shots

Because hitting from the sand is obviously different from hitting off the grass, there are some adjustments you will have to make.

Here are some general suggestions for hitting sand shots that are around the green:

1) Open up the face of your sand wedge by turning it to the right, and then gripping your club.

2) ***Align yourself as you usually do, but with one minor change. Instead of bringing your left foot straight across your body, move it back to create a more open stance.***

3) Your weight will be about 60 percent on your left side.

4) Waggle your feet to set them firmly in the sand. Choke down about one inch on the club to compensate for this.

5) You can use the technique described earlier for the short game (with a ball in your hand, page 62 #4) to determine how far back to take the club.

6) Your swing will be primarily with the shoulders, arms and hands rather than the pelvic area.

Sand Shots

7) ***The beginning of your backswing will be a little different. You want to think more "up and vertical" rather than "rounded."*** Also, you will have a more noticeable sharp break in your wrists on the downswing.

8) One technique for determining the speed when you are in a sand trap near the green is to imagine how hard you would have to swing for the sand to land on the green.

9) For normal, coarse sand you are going to hit about 2 inches behind the ball. Hit down sharply through the sand and follow through.

10) For wet, heavy sand, place more weight on your left side and swing harder. Concentrate on hitting a spot about one inch behind the ball and having a little less of an upright swing.

11) For hard packed sand, use a pitching wedge or 9-iron and swing more upright. Hit the ball cleanly taking as little sand as possible.

12) Practice with the purpose of creating the feel for the plane of your swing and where to hit. With diligent practice, hitting sand shots from around the green can be accomplished easily.

13) *Remember your first priority: Get out of the sand trap!*

Different Ball Positions

The set-ups for most of your golf shots have been discussed earlier. However, there will be certain ball positions in which adjustments will have to be made.

After setting up for the various ball positions described in this section, I found it advantageous to move back about a foot from the ball and take a practice shot. Watch where the clubhead strikes the ground and, if you have to, move your body to the right or left so that the clubhead will strike the ball squarely. Then move directly up into your starting position.

Here are a few ball positions you may encounter:

1) **Uphill Lie (*Your left foot is above the right.*)**
Align your body in the same direction as the slope and to the right of your target.
Place more weight on the right leg.
Use a longer club than the yardage indicates. (For example, use a 6-iron instead of a 7-iron.)
Play the ball farther forward in your stance.
Grip down on the club for better control.
Use a three-quarter backswing and swing up the slope.

2) **Downhill Lie (*Your right foot is above the left.*)**
Align your body in the same direction as the slope and to the left of your target.
Place more weight on the left leg.
Use a shorter club than the yardage indicates.
Play the ball farther back in your stance.
Use a three-quarter backswing and swing down the slope.

3

4

Different Ball Positions

3) **Sidehill Lie (*The ball is below your feet.*)**
Bend your back slightly more forward in your stance.
Aim to the left of the target.
Flex your knees more and increase the width of your stance more for better balance.
Keep your weight on your heels.
Step closer to the ball in your set-up position.
Play the ball slightly forward in your stance.
Make a three-quarter backswing for better control.
Keep your head down through impact.

4) **Sidehill Lie (*The ball is above your feet.*)**
Keep your back slightly more upright in your stance.
Aim to the right of the target.
Use a longer club than the yardage indicates.
Place your weight more on your left side.
Keep your weight on your toes.
Grip down on the club for better control.
Bend from the waist a little more than normal in order to reach the ball.
Play the ball slightly back in your stance.
Make a three-quarter backswing for better control.
Have a smooth tempo on your downswing.

Different Ball Positions

5) ***Hitting Under a Tree***
Use a longer club, like a 3-iron.
Play the ball farther back in your stance.
Place your body weight more on your left side.

6) ***Hitting Over a Tree***
Use a more lofted club, like a 9-iron.
Play the ball farther forward in your stance.
Place your body weight more on your right side.
Your downswing will be more vertical, as it is in a sand trap.

Causes for Bad Shots

1) ***All golfers hit bad shots. But good golfers want to understand why certain shots were bad. And they are dedicated to practicing in order to take the necessary corrective actions.***

I suggest that at one of your practice sessions you consciously hit bad shots to help you understand how and why your shots were bad. You only have to do this once because you don't want to instill in yourself bad habits. For example, you can consciously move your head and shoulders ahead of the ball at impact, or not shift your weight on the downswing. Or you can place the ball too far forward or back in your stance. Observe what happens. *Use your session as a learning experience.*

The most common bad shots discussed in this section are: the slice, the hook, topping, a fat shot, the shank, a pull shot and a push shot.

You will notice that similar causes may exist for various bad shots. Also, corrective actions may involve a combination of the causes for the bad shot.

Remember, the problem may not be with your swing alone, and could very well be with another aspect of your game.

If you continue to have problems, you can have a friend whose opinion you respect evaluate your game, or you might want to take lessons from a professional.

Causes for Bad Shots

The Slice

A slice occurs when the ball starts left and curves sharply to the right.

Possible causes:

1) Your body is misaligned to the left of the target line.

2) Your shoulders are turned to the left in your set-up position.

3) The ball is too far forward in your set-up position.

4) Your clubhead is not aligned squarely with the target line in your set-up position.

5) You grip the club too far to the left (showing too few knuckles) or too tight.

6) ***There is too much lateral movement of the right leg, head and upper body on the backswing.***

7) Your shoulders don't turn properly on the backswing.

8) Your swing path is out-to-in.

9) The clubface is open at impact.

❸

Causes for Bad Shots

The Hook

A hook occurs when the ball starts right and curves sharply to the left.

Possible causes:

1) Your body is misaligned to the right of the target line.

2) Your shoulders are turned to the right in your set-up position.

3) ***The ball is too far back in your set-up position.***

4) Your clubhead is not aligned squarely with the target line in your set-up position.

5) You grip the club too far to the right (showing too many knuckles) or too tight.

6) Your takeaway of the club is too close to the inside of your body.

7) Your swing path is in-to-out.

8) The clubface is closed at impact.

Causes for Bad Shots

Topping

Topping the ball occurs when you strike the ball close to the top with the bottom of the club, rather than the center of the club making contact with the back of the ball.

Possible causes:

1) ***The ball is too far forward in your set-up position.***

2) Your body posture is too crouched over in your set-up position.

3) Your knees are too rigid and not properly flexed.

4) You grip the club too tightly creating tension in your arms and hands.

5) You don't make a complete shoulder turn.

6) Your head and shoulders move upward at impact.

Causes for Bad Shots

A Fat Shot

A fat shot occurs when the club strikes the ground before it strikes the ball.

Possible causes:

1) ***Your body is too close to the ball in your set-up position.***

2) The ball is too far forward in your set-up position.

3) Your body posture is too crouched over in your set-up position.

4) There is too much tension in your arms and hands.

5) You don't turn your shoulders properly on the backswing.

6) Your body weight stays on the right side on the downswing.

7) Your downswing is on too steep of a plane.

8) You slow down your downswing just before impact.

6

Causes for Bad Shots

The Shank

A shank occurs when the ball is struck with the heel of the club and the ball goes sharply to the right almost at a 90 degree angle.

Possible causes:

1) Your body is too close to the ball in your set-up position.

2) Your grip on the club is wrong or too tight.

3) There is too much tension in your arms and hands.

4) You slow down the club on the downswing just before impact.

5) Your clubhead is outside the ball on your downswing.

6) ***Your head and shoulders are ahead of the ball at impact.***

Causes for Bad Shots

A Pull Shot

A pull shot occurs when the shot starts straight to the left and then curves slightly to the left.

Possible causes:

1) Your body is not aligned parallel to the target line in your set-up position.

2) The ball is too far forward in your set-up position.

3) ***Your body posture is too crouched over in your set-up position.***

4) You grip the club too far to the right (showing too many knuckles) or too tight.

5) Your shoulders don't turn properly on the backswing.

6) Your body weight transfer to the left side begins with the upper body and shoulders rather than with your left heel down.

7) The rhythm of your downswing is too fast.

8) The clubface is closed at impact.

1

A Push Shot

A push shot occurs when the shot starts straight to the right and then curves slightly to the right.

Possible causes:

1) ***Your body is not aligned parallel to the target line in your set-up position.***

2) The ball is too far back in your set-up position.

3) You grip the club too far to the left (showing too few knuckles) in your set-up position.

4) Your head and upper body are ahead of the ball at impact.

5) The clubface is open at impact.

Course Management

Here are a few suggestions that helped me prepare to play a course:

1) *It is most important for you to know the exact yardage you will get from each one of your clubs.* Once you know the distance you want to achieve for your shot, you must be confident that the club you choose will provide that distance for you.

2) Choose carefully what clubs to carry in your bag. Select clubs that can get you into a position to be on the green in regulation for every hole. An advanced player, because of the greater distance he or she can drive the ball, may carry more short-game clubs. *However, as a beginner you may decide to carry more long-game clubs and fewer short-game clubs.*

3) You don't necessarily have to go for the greatest distance on each shot. If you are more proficient, for example, in the 150-yard range, you may want to aim for that area rather than the 140-yard area in planning for your next shot onto the green.

4) In windy conditions you may have to use a stronger club (for example, a 3-wood instead of a 5-wood) to achieve the same distance you would get on a normal day.

5) ***Tee up your ball on the trouble side.*** If there is water on the right, tee up the ball on the right side.

8

Course Management

6) If you are in deep rough or against an obstacle such as a tree, your first priority is to get the ball back onto the fairway.

7) Know the position of the flag in order to get your correct yardage to the hole. Some greens can be 30-40 yards long from the front of the green to the back.

8) ***Visualize your shots.***

9) Know yourself and what works best for you. Also, learn from each shot. Understand why certain shots of yours were good and also why others were not so good.

10) Use whatever techniques enable you to get your ball into the hole.

11) *Remember the good shots*. Leave the course remembering the shots you executed with excellence.

Practice with Intention

To get the most out of your practice sessions you should have a pre-determined plan of what you want to accomplish.

1) If you have just completed a round of golf and there was a segment of your game, or a club, that gave you problems, then that is what you want to give your immediate attention to when practicing.

2) You may find that for a particular club you are using there is a significant checkpoint which helps you to perform better with that club. For example, for a driver it may be having your back to the target, while for a 9-iron it may be your rhythm and for your putting it may be eyes over the ball. Give each of these checkpoints special attention in your practice sessions.

3) One way to practice is to take a scorecard from the next golf course you will be playing and play each hole on the practice range. Look at the distance of the hole and use the same club that you would use on the course. Judge the distance of your shot and then select the next club accordingly. When you feel you are on the green, give yourself two putts and move on to the next hole.

4) ***You can even practice inside your house.*** Take an old club to an equipment shop and have the shaft cut down to two feet. Use the club inside the house to practice your swing.

Practice with Intention

You can also go out alone on a golf course in the late afternoon when the course is not crowded and play a couple of golf balls. This can be good for your short game in terms of getting a feel for how far back to take your swing and how far the ball rolls on the green.

On the practice range always select a target for your shot to give yourself the feel for playing on a course.

Here are a few suggestions (putting practice will be discussed in the next section of the book) for what you can focus on in a practice session:

1) Your alignment.

2) Your head behind the ball.

3) ***Following through to the finish of your swing.***

4) Turning your back to the target.

5) Your left heel down first on the downswing.

6) Your rhythm.

7) Your grip.

8) Visualizing your shots.

9) Using your pelvis area in your swing.

PUTTING

Putting is the most important part of the game of golf!!!

The winners of tournaments usually one-putt nine of the holes and two-putt the other nine. To excel at golf you must make the time to practice and develop your putting skills to their fullest.

Although there are some fundamentals to the putting game which seem to be universal, this is truly the most individual part of the game. You have to develop your own style and to know what works best for you.

The following are some suggestions as to what you might incorporate into your putting game.

1) Develop a routine. This will be slightly different from your other pre-shot routine and could be the following:

a) Stand behind the ball and visualize an imaginary target line along which you want the ball to travel. Notice how the green is sloped — especially around the hole area. One technique for determining the slope around the hole is to imagine the hole overfilled with water. In which direction will the water be flowing out of the hole?

b) Check out the slope again from the opposite side of the hole looking back to your ball and also walk the two sides of the hole.

PUTTING

c) Align your body parallel to your target line.

d) Place the clubhead square to your target line.

e) You can grip the club the same as you do for your other golf shots.

f) The wrists are locked.

g) Place your left foot to the left so that the ball will be just inside your foot. Place your right foot inside your right shoulder.

h) Be comfortable and relaxed.

i) Your head is still and your eyes are over the ball.

j) The hands, arms and shoulders move together as one. The hands are slightly ahead of the ball with the right hand executing the stroke and the left hand moving in unison with the right.

k) Take two practice strokes.

l) Think "in the hole" no matter what the distance.

m) Step up and execute your stroke.

PUTTING

2) *As a beginner you are encouraged to experiment with different putting styles to determine what works best for you.*

There are numerous putting styles from which to choose. They vary from the "pendulum" method in which the swing is similar to the rhythmic back and forth motion of the pendulum in a clock, to "croquet" style in which you stand facing the putting line and putt between your legs.

3) To settle on a particular style for your putting game, talk to many professional and non-professional golfers as to what method works best for them.

4) There are also many different types of putters to select from. Choose one that feels right for you.

5) ***To be successful at putting you will need to develop the ability to read the greens.*** Though this can be a complex process, you can become proficient at it through your practice sessions.

6) Poorly judged speed is one of the main reasons for missed putts. Controlling your speed is a skill that you should constantly work on and improve.

7) Remember that it is the feel for distance that separates the good putters from the not-so-good.

8) ***One method for measuring the distance of your putts is to walk in three-foot steps.*** Three feet is the approximate length of most putters. Take these three-foot steps to determine your distance from the hole.

9) In reading the greens on seaside courses, remember that the grain will take the ball toward the ocean.

10) In mountainous areas the ball will roll away from the mountain.

11) In short putts of less than six feet concentrate more on speed and less on distance.

12) Inside of three feet don't play the ball on a line outside the hole. By increasing the speed you can hit through the break.

13) The faster a putt rolls, the less it will break. The slower a putt rolls, the more it will break.

14) If you can't read the break, then aim within the hole.

15) *Think like a winner. Have the attitude that you can make any putt.*

Putting Practice

1) To develop your ability to swing the club back and forward in a straight line, place two clubs on the ground parallel to each other, and slightly more than the width of the putter head apart. Stroke the ball without touching the clubs.

2) Enhance your distance control by placing five balls in a straight line at distances of 10, 15, 20, 25 and 30 feet.

Putting Practice

1) For better hand control, you can putt using only your right hand on the club. Then try using only your left hand on the club.

2) For head control, putt and then keep your head down without looking up to see the direction of your putt.

Putting Practice

1) To gain confidence for your long putts, place balls at distances of 35, 40, 45 and 50 feet. Try to keep your misses to within three feet of the hole.

2) To cultivate a better sense of feel and touch, putt with your eyes closed.

Putting Practice

1) To improve your accuracy and concentration place a quarter on the green and use it as your target, instead of the hole. Practice doing this from both close and far distances.

2) To improve your ability to read the slopes of the green, place four balls on a circular path around the hole, with each ball three feet from the hole. After you have putted each ball into the hole, move the balls back another foot from the hole.

Inner Golf

This is the most personalized aspect of golf, the one which you already possess and bring with you to your game.

Don't trivialize this important aspect of the game by thinking in terms of outside "golf gods" who may have been good or not good to you on a particular round of golf.

Just as in your daily life you have developed an inner world and source of guidance, take that same awareness with you into your game of golf.

Clear your mind between shots and ask for guidance, and then listen to that inner voice which will tell you what adjustments to make, what clubs to use or what strategy to employ.

Discover the intimate source of guidance within yourself and then continue that relationship on the golf course. Have fun combining your inner world with the outside world of golf.

Developing your vast inner world is an integral component of golf magic. Allow it to be real for you.

Vocabulary

Splendid, Spectacular, Fabulous, Phenomenal, Magnificent, Marvelous, Astounding, Superb, Brilliant, DAZZLING, Beautiful, Amazing, Impressive, OUTSTANDING, Great, STUPENDOUS, Awesome, Fantastic, Exceptional, Incredible, Remarkable, Sensational, Astonishing, Extraordinary, Unbelievable, Excellent, Terrific, Stunning, Incomparable, Smashing, Exquisite, Memorable, Tremendous, Breathtaking, Miraculous, MAGICAL

Vocabulary

The English language is rich in words that can be used to describe a great shot in golf. Don't hesitate to use them to compliment the shot of someone with whom you are playing.

In addition to the suggestions of words on the opposite page, you can combine these words with a foreign word that means "very."

In Italian "very" is "molto"; in German "sehr"; in French "tres"; and in Japanese "totemo."

Life as Golf

Playing golf can provide you with an excellent opportunity for putting into practice the many universal truths, values, ideals and principles that are a part of your everyday life.

Let's look at some of these and see how they can be adapted to playing golf:

Responsibility

At every turn of events in your world, you must be accountable for the way you are conducting your life according to the choices and decisions you have made. You must also take total responsibility for how your golf game develops, because there is no one else to blame if you are not achieving what you desire.

Self-Image

The way in which you see yourself is the core of the image you convey to your fellow human beings and the interactions that take place between you and others. As you proceed in playing golf, continue to gain knowledge of the game, seeing yourself as a winner while maintaining your sense of self-respect and self-worth.

Acceptance

It is important that you develop a willingness to see things as they really are in your daily life, rather than trying to imagine them as they could have been. Accept your progress or lack thereof graciously as you move forward to strive to achieve your goals in golf.

Laughter

Remember that one of the purposes of your human existence is to have fun. Look for the light side in all aspects of your golf game and develop the ability to laugh at your shortcomings.

Honesty

No matter what circumstances you may find yourself facing in your daily life, be honest, even if it is not always in your best interest. When you're playing golf, you must always play by the rules.

Moment to Moment

Seize each precious moment and appreciate it, for every moment represents the totality of your accumulated experiences and your future aspirations. When you are ready to execute a golf shot, be focused on the present moment and give it your undivided attention.

Beliefs

Beliefs are the framework upon which you build your future and are the foundation for the shape your life will take from this point onward. Examine the beliefs you hold about yourself as a golfer and change those which do not empower you or which prevent you from realizing your full potential.

Trust

Trusting yourself in all of your daily encounters enables you to continuously renew your life and to move forward with confidence. In golf, once you have set-up properly, you must have complete trust in your ability to execute the shot exactly the way you wish.

Viewpoint

Each experience in your life is an opportunity for growth, as long as you are willing to see it as such. What separates success from failure in golf is the way in which you perceive the possibilities inherent in all of your circumstances.

Expectations

Always expect the very best in everything you wish to accomplish in life. You must set high goals for what you hope to achieve in golf, and truly expect to reach them.

Thoughts

Your thoughts are among the principal sources of power and they can determine the measure of success you can have in working through any conflict. Be cognizant of the thoughts you hold about yourself and your golf game, and transform any negative thoughts you may have into positive ones so as not to impede your progress.

Autosuggestion

Your imagination is certainly one of the most profound of your natural resources and it links together the subconscious and conscious dimensions of your thoughts. What you visualize — both on the golf course and in your private meditations — can condition to a great degree the way in which your game will actually be played out.

Learning

Each experience in your life represents the gaining of new information to be used in your development as an individual and as a successful member of society. Each time you practice or play a round of golf, you should seek to learn from that experience and make it the groundwork for your future playing.

Feelings

Your feelings represent the way in which you react to your perception of the world around you, and as such, are fundamental indicators of what you understand to be the truth. As you progress in playing golf, maintain the positive feelings you have about yourself and your game, and change all other feelings concerning your ability to play into positive energies.

GOLF
MAGIC
GOLF MAGIC
1

The Magic

Whether or not you choose to acknowledge it, you are already in possession of the magic.

Golf magic begins when you take the magic already within you and apply it to the game of golf.

You may not be able to fully understand your personal magic. Its deeper meaning truly lies within the realm of mystery. The magic is a synergy. It contains all of your power and resources and yet it is something more.

You do know, however, when you have experienced it. Think of the times when your dreams became a reality, combining your talents with the power of your will and imagination. The magic can also be found in the ecstasy of your peak experiences or in the quiet enchantment of your solitary moments.

Your magic has no boundaries. The understanding and pursuit of magic is a life-long experience because it is a never-ending process.

If this book has served as a spark to assist you in beginning or continuing the process of discovering your own personal magic, then it surely will have accomplished its purpose of helping you to be more successful at – and to have more fun playing – golf.

It is hoped that as you continue on your golf journey—***the magic only increases***.

Printed in the United States
41647LVS00007B/190